How to save the world and
have a better life than you ever imagined!

John Z. Molly

I0463826

Contents

Chapter 1:
Introduction

Good news, finally there is a practical plan to fix everything, and you can be an important part of it.

This can benefit everybody including you and everyone you care about.

This is not going to happen by itself. If you have ever wanted to do something really important and long lasting, this is your chance. We need you.

Realistic

This is completely realistic because an idea can spread all over the world and change everything.

As an example, they used to use the barter system, then somebody had an idea to invent currency, and now currency is used everywhere. That currency idea spread all over the world and resulted in major changes.

Some of those changes may be of questionable value, but the point remains that ideas do spread all over, therefore the ideas in this book can very well accomplish the stated goals.

Fortunately the ideas in this book are all good.

The ideas in this book can spread all over and fix everything.

There are a lot of other reasons why this can succeed, but this is just the introduction chapter, so only a summary is presented here.

Why this is so important

A lot of possible problems are pending in the near future, and the ideas in this book are the only way to fix the problems.

Also, a lot of people are suffering through no fault of their own. There is no reason a child should starve or suffer in any way.

But this book is not only about ending the suffering. It is also about having a much better or more productive life. Even if things are good now, what if you could be having an even better life? Why settle for second best?

A lot of people are having a life that is so excellent that it is unbelievable right now. Don't you want to have a better life too?

A new era for humanity

Society has seen many improvements. Every once in a while, a new era begins, with major changes for humanity.

For example, people used to be hunters and gatherers, then somebody introduced farming, which is more efficient. This allows more time to work on other things.

Then the industrial revolution and assembly line resulted in a lot of people having access to phones and all those other things.

The ideas in this book will usher in the next big change in society.

This will start the next era for humanity, which will result in the system of the future, where everybody has an excellent life.

Disclaimer

Nothing in this book should be used as legal advice, medical advice, or any other kind of professional advice. Information is provided on an as is basis, with no liability for use or misuse. For academic use only. Company names, trademarks, or any other words are used in an editorial way with no infringement intended. If a company name, trademark, or any other term is mentioned, this in no way implies that the company or organization has endorsed the ideas mentioned in this publication. Everything in this book is an expression of opinion of the author.

Chapter 2:
Decentralization

The internet is decentralized for good reasons.

If the internet wasn't decentralized, then all the data would be going through a central computer, and every time that computer had a problem, the whole internet would be down.

That doesn't happen because the internet is decentralized, so any problems are usually limited in size. Obviously there is an exception to every rule, but the point remains that the internet does have a good track record as of the time this book was written. That good track record would not have happened without decentralization.

It may not be perfect, but it does have clear advantages over every other system.

The world

We need to use decentralization to fix the worlds problems.

The only way we can succeed is to have enough people. But if we try to have one large global group, then it would likely become a bureaucratic mess, or have some other problems, and it would fail to save the world.

Yet if we have a lot of groups pulling in different directions, that would fail too.

We can avoid all those problems by having decentralized groups all joined by an alliance. This has a lot of advantages that are explained in this book.

Avoiding mistakes

Some previous attempts to improve things have failed because they tried to have a one size fits all. If there is a problem, and there usually is, then the problem is everywhere. Nobody wants that.

We absolutely must avoid repeating the mistakes of the past.

The world needs to be decentralized, with each region running things in a manner that is helpful and good for the people living there. Yet each region is still part of a larger team, with all the associated benefits. We need that teamwork, it is essential for our success, and it is lacking in the world today.

Chapter 3:
The alliance, introduction

Some previous attempts to fix the worlds problems have failed because they did not have enough people.

This book advocates forming a global alliance of all the good groups. This alliance would be so large that it would be certain to succeed.

There are real advantages to having one global alliance of groups, all working for a common goal. Synergy is one of the advantages.

It can be difficult to persuade groups to join an alliance, but there are many ways to accomplish this goal.

Most people like the goals of this book, and will be happy to be a part of the alliance.

If we do it right, this alliance will have enough people to fix everything.

Name

We will have to come up with a better name for the alliance, but for now this book will simply refer to it as the alliance.

Fringe benefit

This book has two goals, to end all unnecessary suffering, and to ensure everyone has an excellent life.

It is questionable if enough people or groups would join an alliance for the purpose of ending world suffering. But almost everyone would love a stronger economy, more money, and other things.

To solve this problem, to make sure we get enough people to accomplish all the goals of this book, we can make the alliance primarily for having a better life, and we end the suffering as a fringe benefit.

These goals are related, and the same plan that accomplishes one will accomplish the other too.

Chapter 4:
What you can do to help

There are a lot of things you can do, mentioned in various points in this book.

This chapter is just a summary of some quick things.

Ideas

If you have any good ideas that will help to save the world, then you can tell them to a group that is in the alliance. It is far more likely your idea will get noticed if you are part of a group, and you get the group to help promote it.

If you are not part of a group, then your idea might get ignored and go nowhere. A lot of cases of this have happened in the past.

Groups

Another thing you could do, if you are a member of any good group, is to try to get the group to join the alliance. Explain the benefits of synergy, or any of the other ideas in this book, to the group.

If enough members of the group agree, then the group will likely join the alliance, so we can begin to get enough people to succeed.

Since the alliance has not been officially formed as of the time this book was written, the groups can start by stating that they support the proposal in this book and at www.endworldsuffering.org which will allow us to keep in contact until we work out the details. The website will post news and information as progress starts to be made. The group should also write a brief description of the importance of teamwork, so everyone will see why it's so important to be part of this team.

Realistic

A lot of good groups have formed over the years. They try to accomplish their goal, but the goal only appeals to a certain percentage of the population, and it never gets majority support. It never accomplishes its goal.

If you are a member of such a group, but want a better future for it, then the only way to succeed is to get the group to join the alliance. This way it will be part of such a large alliance that it can accomplish its goal.

This is assuming that its goal is good, and it fits with the goals of this book and the alliance.

The only realistic way to accomplish anything is to have enough people, and that is where the alliance comes in. A large global alliance has enough people to accomplish goals. A small group often does not.

Chapter 5:
Summary of the plan

This quick summary leaves out a lot of important details, but since not everyone has the time to read the whole book, it might be helpful to have a summary here.

Beginning

We can start by having a meeting with all the good groups that like the ideas in this book. Every group can send one or more members to this meeting.

The author will help them officially form an alliance, and make sure that it is for the benefit of the people.

We can decide upon a better name for the alliance, maybe by having a contest, this way it can be something that everybody likes.

Some group members can be part of the alliance, and help it get started. The alliance can work to get more groups to join it, so it grows large enough to accomplish our goals.

It can do this by news interviews, or calling groups and inviting them, or any other ideas they develop.

The author will write about more ideas, and work with the alliance closely to ensure a brighter future for humanity.

One approach

One possible strategy would be to identify a section of land that has problems, and focus the attention of the alliance on fixing it.

By pooling resources, we could fix all the problems in this small section of land, setting up everything the people need to have an excellent and sustainable life.

All the ideas of this book would be implemented, so the people of this land would never have any problems in the future.

This land would become a region in the alliance.

Then the alliance moves on to another section of land, fixing the problems there.

Eventually the entire earth is converted into an excellent place to live, and it is sustainable so it stays that way forever. No more problems.

Economy

A new economic system is introduced later in this book. This will be very helpful in making everything better.

The rest

There is a lot more than has been mentioned in this summary.

Some details are mentioned in the rest of the chapters of this book.

There are a lot more exceptionally good ideas that are necessary to our success, that the author will write about, once the alliance is formed.

Chapter 6
Better housing

A lot of the problems of the world are resulting from bad housing. Examples include fires, noise from neighbors, and earthquakes causing people to be crushed from the collapse.

These problems are easily avoided with the futuristic housing proposal detailed in this chapter.

There are a lot of variations of this idea, but they all have advantages over the old style housing. One variation has a conventional look, but is still high density. All variations will likely have high technology built in.

Proposal

We could make a building complex around a beautiful park in the center full of green plants. Residences and jobs are all nearby so you could walk to work by going through the park.

If the weather is bad, you could use the windowed walkways that connect the buildings. No more going out in the cold or rain.

This is a great way to stay healthy by walking, and we avoid the commute and all those expenses.

Everything you find in a city would be in this complex, all conveniently located nearby. No more long commute, no more wasted time.

Or take your car parked right in front of the building, and drive around the outside of the complex.

The complex would only be a few stories high, but would cover a large area, so everybody would have quick access to the nearest door, and there would be plenty of free parking spaces available for everybody.

There are more than enough parking places because a complex with a huge park in the center, has a parking space right in front of each housing unit. Imagine a building complex 1 mile or about 2 kilometers in diameter, how much space would be available on the perimeter of such a complex. The majority of the center is a park with nobody living there, so people only live near the outer edge of this complex. You could look out the window and your car would be right there.

Electric cars would be very practical since you don't have to go very far (only minimal battery power is needed).

There should be a monorail type system within the complex, which has a lot of small cars, so you don't have to share a car with a stranger if you don't want to. This is a lot better than the typical public transport.

There have been a lot of movies about the future, showing a wide variety of advanced transport systems. There is no reason we can't make one of those systems for this building.

And of course you can always walk outside the building or take a shortcut through the park in the center.

There should be a lot of these buildings, so some buildings can be different, and everybody can select which building and transport system they prefer. Some buildings can look conventional, some like a spaceship, and some can have other designs.

Everybody doesn't have to live in these buildings. Some people prefer other housing, and that is fine. But a lot of people would like the benefits of this type of housing, and so it should be made available to anyone who wants it.

Benefits

You could literally save thousands of Euro/Dollars/Pounds by avoiding car expenses if you choose to use the monorail system which is free like the elevator/lift in most buildings.

This can easily save you twenty thousand Euro/Dollars/Pounds over a few years.

Don't believe the cost savings? Add up the purchase price of a car, fuel, insurance, maintenance, etc and multiply by a few years.

The time savings are also significant. As a high density structure, you don't have to waste a lot of time commuting to work.

Safety is the best benefit.

Safety

The building should be made like a cruise ship, in other words, from steel. Why? Because it doesn't collapse like concrete, during an earthquake. It is very strong, if you build it properly.

Look at news archives showing what happens to a lot of buildings during earthquakes if you want to see why this is so important. Read about people who have had limbs amputated to free them from the collapsed wreckage.

They all thought it would never happen to them; these things only happen to other people.

We need to start making these advanced buildings so it never happens to anybody.

I do realize that current construction is resistant to earthquakes, it just seems like we could have an extra measure of safety.

If it is built properly, steel or other metal has absolutely no problems. It can be insulated so it is a good temperature all the time, and it lasts a long time. More evidence can be observed in the housing that is currently being built from old steel shipping containers.

A lot of buildings are already made from steel, and you can't always tell by looking since they can be made to look like any style.

Steel buildings, along with sensible furnishings and everything else, let us avoid the senseless fire deaths that happen every year.

When I talk about fireproof furnishings I don't mean the type of furniture that has toxic chemicals in it that some places have already banned due to possible health problems. There are better ways.

Details

This complex would have everything you need. This includes the residences for each person or family, and has so many rooms that anybody who wants their own room can have one.

The walls in this building are soundproof so you can listen to music without complaints from anybody else, yet you can always have it quiet whenever you want.

This is exceptionally high quality housing.

The complex also has workplaces, a galley or other eating places, a gym, and more.

All kinds of advanced technology can be built into this building. It could be powered by renewable energy.

The only thing that would not be in this complex is any company that works with hazardous materials or anything else that is not suitable for a residential area. Those companies will have to be located far away from this building.

Cost

Another problem with housing of today, is that it is so expensive that people often can't afford high quality housing.

Later in this book we will see how regional competition fixes this problem, so everybody can afford good quality housing.

Exclusive housing

Many people don't want to live in a city. So some of these buildings can be suburb or rural models.

Priority

There should be no delays for the first building, we should design and build it as soon as possible.

Perhaps this first building can serve as the office for the alliance, so members can live in the building and enjoy the benefits.

Chapter 7:
Regions

You will probably hate this, but there are so many benefits that it should be considered a key part of this project.

Summary

What if the land was divided into regions, and each region had to compete to do the best job for the people who choose to live there?

Each region is managed by a different organization.

After some time, we look at which regions are the best places to live.

If a region is not an excellent place to live, then that region gets managed by one of the other organizations that is doing an excellent job.

This type of competition would fix most of the problems. All regions will become great places to live.

There are different ways of implementing this, but they all result in everything getting better.

Competition always results in improvements wherever it is used. Why don't we start using it in regional management too?

Differences

There are some important differences between regions and the current system.

One major difference is regions don't have to compromise all the time.

The current system is constantly full of compromises such as when one political party has to compromise with another party, when making laws, and both sides lose something they wanted.

With regions, one region could be run by one party, and do most things their way, and another region could be run by the other party and mostly do things their way.

This could start small, with regions being built on undeveloped land and volunteers move there to enjoy the benefits. It would only expand slowly, as more people want to get the benefits.

Problems

There are a number of different ways to do this, but to keep this book a reasonable size, only the basics are mentioned. So if you see a problem, you can rest assured that it will be fixed during the meetings of the alliance. We will discuss the details and options, to decide upon the best way to proceed.

Then we will start small and expand gradually so it does not cause any problems to the existing system. As it helps the economy, it will become more popular and continue to grow.

If you would like to help, then please join one of the groups in the alliance so you can be involved in all this.

People first

Right now, companies put profits first, people second.

Once this new system of regions is finished, people will come first.

It really is that good. This is the way of the future.

People will be first because any organization that fails to do that, will get replaced by one of the superior organizations that does put people first. After a while, there will be no bad organizations remaining.

One team

These regions will all be part of the same team, even though each region "mostly" does things its own way with regards to local control.

People

It is difficult or impossible to get everybody to go along with a different system, but we can build new regions on undeveloped land and let volunteers move there to prove the new system.

Then as the news reports how good everything is in these regions, more people will want to use the new system, and it can expand.

Then some existing towns and cities can join in, because the people living there will want to get the benefits too.

Entirety

This concept of regions is complex and has a lot of details and options, so the only way to see the benefits is to read this entire book. That is the only way that everything will tie in together. Until the entire book is read, regions may not make much sense.

Competition

Competition is the reason that stores or shops usually don't have shortages of products.

What if competition was used in other aspects of life, including government?

Competition has always resulted in improvements. Imagine a society free from job shortages.

Imagine getting a better job, or better housing or other benefits!

The existing system is doing a poor job at improving everybodys life. Even if it is great in your area, it's not like that for the rest of us.

Regions plan

The plan is to divide land into economic regions that have to compete to improve everything.

All regions are still part of the same team (the alliance).

This starts small, and some of the regions are managed by nonprofit organizations or other groups instead of the local government.

All regions compete with each other to do a better job for the people. Everybody votes on which region is better.

If a region is popular, like it has a better economy and more jobs, then that region gets to manage more land.

If a region has a job shortage and nobody votes for it, then that land gets managed by one of the better regions and so it becomes part of a popular region, with plenty of jobs and other benefits.

Each region has to compete to do the best job for the people who choose to live there.

This kind of competition will quickly result in all regions getting better. It is a business friendly environment, so we get a stronger economy.

Everything will get better because of this type of competition, it is not just about jobs or the economy.

If the organization running a region wants to stay in business, then it has to do a good job, else it goes out of business and a better organization gets to manage that land.

Obviously there are a lot of details needed to make this work, but the basics are all figured out already.

The bottom line is that competition will improve everything, as it always does.

The first country to implement these economic regions will see it's economy improve tremendously! Then other countries will want to follow it.

Advantages

One advantage of these regions is that we can implement a different system in a new town built from scratch, without trying to get the majority in an existing town to try something different.

This is probably the only way to get started with a different system because it is usually impossible to get the majority to go along with something new. At least until they see the new system working great, then they will become more interested in it.

It is important to try new and different systems because some of them will be better than the existing system.

The existing system is not going to get better on its own, as we have seen repeatedly, with the high unemployment rates, and other problems.

Innovations

The benefits of competition are well documented.

This kind of competition will quickly result in innovations that you would never see with todays system.

Practical

There are a lot of reasons that this is completely workable.

We will find a way to solve any petty problems that arise, and develop this into a working system.

Some people will see a problem with this new system, and promptly give up, without even trying to fix it. The rest of us will find a way to fix it, and make it into the best system that benefits everyone.

Support

If anybody questions if there is enough support for changes like this, let's remember the Quebec referendum of 1995 when they wanted to separate from Canada.

It was a very close vote, 49.4% to 50.6%, indicating a very strong support for independence.

A lot of people already want changes, in one form or another.

This regions plan can get a higher percentage of support because all regions are still part of the same team therefore there are no concerns related to complete independence.

In other words, regions are the best of both worlds. They combine all the benefits and none of the drawbacks of other past ideas. We get enough independence to live as we see fit, yet we also keep the benefits of teamwork.

There are a lot of other reasons why regions can get enough support to work.

A lot of people already want a new or better system.

And there is the humanitarian aspect, which should be enough reason by itself.

Details

Regional competition (regions competing with each other) is a concept similar to retail stores/shops.

If one store/shop doesn't give good sales prices, or a good variety of products, then nobody shops there because there are better choices. Stores all improve because of competition, and everybody benefits.

Competition doesn't work with the type of cities and towns we have now, partly because there is very little local control. Most rules are national or international.

Also, if people move out, the land stays with the same system and its faulty economy; nothing changes.

There is no real competition, no new systems.

Its the same race to the bottom, and it isn't going to get better unless we adopt this new system of competition.

Regions competing with each other is the same as stores competing with each other. They improve themselves to serve you better. Everything in your life would get better because of this type of regional competition.

This book does not explain all the details and benefits. The alliance will put together a much better presentation, including videos, that does a great job of explaining all the benefits. This book is more like a getting started guide.

Leaders

It is possible for the same people to be in charge, as we have now, so we can still have experienced people running things.

Local control

For regions to be able to work, they need local control.

Everything starts small, so they are still part of the country they are located in, and thus don't have any more say in foreign policy than every other city in the country.

But they do need local control, otherwise it isn't a region. Regions make their own local laws. Laws are not imposed on them from afar. This local control is one of the main reasons that regions will improve everything for you.

One of the reasons we have problems today is too much bureaucracy, too many unnecessary rules, not enough freedom to innovate.

The first regions will need to be located in countries that will allow for this local control.

A prospective region can have some laws imposed by the nation or province, only while it is getting started, as per the concept of phasing this in slowly and gradually.

But it is not a full region until the only laws in the region are the ones made by the people of that region, via whatever organization is running that region.

Some regulations make sense, and we will still have all of those. But other regulations are frivolous and counterproductive, made by the uninformed, and we need the ability to reform all those counterproductive rules.

Of course basic human rights still apply everywhere, in all regions. An example is the right to move out of the region; everybody has the basic human right to move out of the region if they wish.

Conflict

Today, companies face a conflict between doing what's best for profit, or what's best for the people. Guess which one wins.

This is why companies lay off people and leave them unemployed for a long time. Its profitable.

Regions have no conflict, they are for the people because people decide which regions stay in business or not.

So all regions get better and better, they race to the top, to serve you the best quality of life.

Companies work for profit; regions work for you. Which one do you think will give you more opportunities and a better life?

For you

Right now, companies compete to make the most profit, which is good for them.

Regions compete to do the best job for the people who choose to live there, which is good for you.

Every organization running a region will have to do a good job for the people, else the organization goes out of business, and the land gets managed by a better organization that does a better job for you and everybody in the region.

Jobs

Regions will not be able to ignore people like the old fashioned society does, with respect to an insufficient number of jobs.

If a region tried that, then a better region would come along that has more jobs.

The better region would become a more popular region.

Then other regions would have to improve themselves to keep up with the competition, and everything gets better everywhere.

Simplified

This is a rather simplified explanation, maybe not the best description, but it may be helpful.

You may have noticed that some countries have a strong economy and some don't. But everybody can't just move to one country that has a good economy.

What regions do is allow the country to move to the people, so to speak. In other words the region with the good economy expands, it manages more land, so the goodness comes to the people. This way people don't have to move, yet they get the benefits of the better system.

Again, this is not the best description, it leaves out a lot of details and options, but it might be helpful in understanding the benefits of the regional competition.

Determining popularity

There are a number of different ways we could determine which region is popular and gets to manage more land.

If everybody moved out of a region then the organization running it goes out of business, and the land is given to one of the better regions.

However it is impractical to expect everybody to move, therefore we can use other methods like voting to determine the popularity of each region, and how much land each region gets.

One possibility is that every person gets one vote, and every region gets an amount of land proportional to the number of votes.

So if a region gets 2% of the vote then it gets 2% of the land. People do not actually have to move to the region they voted for, but would be able to do so if they wish.

This system is fair because by giving regions the amount of land proportional to their popularity, we get rid of unpopular regions, resulting in the best service to the people.

Regions will most likely offer to pay moving expenses to get people to move to that region, because regions get more land as they get more people. Land is bought and sold every day already, so this is not really as much of a problem as it may sound.

The exact method of determining popularity of a region can be determined later, when we form an official organization. We may use a combination of votes and the actual number of people living in the region. There are other options too. The obvious problems with all this will be discussed and fixed during the meetings, and it really is possible to fix the problems so that this works very well.

The main point is that all regions will improve because of the competition, so most people will not have to move to get the benefits. Everything will get better at your location.

Government competition

In many parts of the world today, the government postal mail (snail mail) service has to compete with private companies offering overnight letter and package delivery.

Before the private companies started, the government had no competition so they had no express (overnight or 2 day delivery) options. They also had no tracking of lost packages.

Then private companies started offering fast shipping and tracking options, which is a lot better especially if you are running a business and need these services.

Then the government mail started improving itself to stay somewhat competitive.

This example is discussed to point out the viability of regions. Government and private companies are already competing in some areas, so there is no reason not to expand it into other areas and get the benefits from it.

Economic sustainability of regions

One of the reasons we want to do this is to avoid the periodic recessions that cause so many problems for people. Every so often, another recession causes many people to lose their jobs, get evicted from their houses, etc.

Regions ideally should all be economically sustainable, in other words they provide for all the people all the time, forever.

Each region will likely have its own system, but all systems should provide for everybody.

We can do this in a decentralized way by letting competition work. In other words, people will want to live in a region where they have security and stability, so all regions will provide it in one way or another.

The goal is to have a system where nobody is ever laid off from work and evicted from their home, and the type of regional competition in this book can give that to everyone.

The other ideas that will be mentioned later, all contribute to making this practical enough to really work.

Specialized regions

Around half the population may want to do something, and the other half wants it banned.

The old fashioned way society handles this is to make one side lose, or there is a compromise in which case both sides lose.

Regions solve this problem by having one region allow it, and the other region doesn't. Everybody wins.

This is one of the most important benefits of regions, the ability for everybody to have the level of freedom they want, while not being around something they are uncomfortable with.

Geographical separation can be used where needed. In other words an island or continent can have one system, and it is physically separate from the other system.

Continents can also be subdivided by fences or nature reserves, and there are a lot of other options.

We would need to allow everybody to move to whatever region they want, even across continents
(Exclusive regions are OK if you don't want people moving into your area).

But look at the benefits.

Banning things is often wrong because it either doesn't work, or it makes things worse, or it is unfair to the half of the population that wants it and is using it in a responsible manner.

It didn't work during the prohibition of alcohol.

Everybody drank anyway, and it made it worse because the alcohol was illegally made and much of it was contaminated, resulting in blindness and other problems.

Far better to let everybody choose a region with like minded people, who want to live the same way, and have no motive to disobey the laws.

Freedom is important.

We need the freedom to live in a region of our choice.

It is very disturbing that some people want to force their way of living on everybody else, like some kind of outdated dictator. Far better to have a thousand regions, each one different, so everybody can choose the one that is best for them.

For example if somebody doesn't like alcohol, they can live in a dry region where everybody feels the same way. This way they can avoid being around alcohol without taking the freedom away from other people.

Alcohol may be a bad example but the point remains that banning everything is unfair. More about this later.

Another way to look at it

Everybody has the right to move to whatever region they want, except some exclusive regions that restrict immigration.

You can still have an exclusive region that restricts immigration if you prefer to not have anybody moving into your area.

Regions have the consent of the governed, the will of the people, since everybody can choose which region they want to live in, and the laws of that region.

Contrast this with the old fashioned system of today, where many people do not consent, but are unable to do anything about it, for example when they vote against something but lose to the uninformed majority.

Some regions will make it easy for people to move in, so now everybody has more choices.

Since every region is populated only by people who actually want to live there, the regions have consent of the governed. This is a milestone for freedom, and will result in a much better life for billions of people.

Even people who don't care about freedom will benefit from this, since they no longer have to compromise with everybody else in their area. They can have a region with like minded people, and not have to be around anything they are uncomfortable with.

Freedom regions

Specialized regions are one of the best things about this plan.

Even if everything is going great in your part of the world, it is not necessarily like that for the rest of us. So if you would please help this get started then the rest of us would really appreciate your help.

Freedom is rapidly diminishing in many parts of the world. This is unacceptable to huge numbers of good responsible people.

These plans would result in freedom regions where we could regain our lost freedoms.

If somebody doesn't like a particular freedom, they can live in one of the regions that doesn't allow that particular freedom. This is a lot better than the present system that currently allows some of the freedom that the person is uncomfortable with.

Right now, some freedoms are available in a limited way. Compromise has resulted in a situation that both sides don't like; regions solves this problem.

Before anybody suggests that the banned item would be smuggled into a region that doesn't allow it, remember that the only people living in such a region are the ones that don't want that item, therefore there is no incentive to smuggle anything.

The main point here is that regions give everybody the opportunity for a better life. A lot of good people want this better life.

Would you like to have more rights than you have today?

Proportional land

Today, land is bought and sold all the time.

For regions to be most effective, they have to lose land if people move out, because this provides a serious incentive to keep things good for the people.

If a region has one percent of the population, then it should have one percent of the land. This is fair.

It keeps popular regions from getting overcrowded, since they would get more land as more people moved in.

Land is bought and sold every day already, so this is not really as big a problem as it might sound.

But bear in mind that regional competition will result in all regions getting better, so most people really won't have to move.

Better life for you

The free market system has resulted in a lot of services and consumer products, some of which improve life.

Unfortunately a lot of people can't afford everything they want, because the economy is slow, because there is no real competition in the form of regional competition.

Another problem is limitations, laws that unfairly restrict freedom in some parts of the world.

There are a lot of other problems that result in a lesser lifestyle.

Regions fix all these problems, because they allow new systems with more freedom, and have a better economy so people can afford what they want.

Whatever you want, it is highly likely that regions will provide it for you, because regions have to compete and only the best ones stay in business.

Competition does things like this.

It results in innovations that you would never see in any other system.

It is our only chance for a better future.

Regions will provide a better life than you could have imagined!

Housing

Ideally, housing should be provided free for all. How is this practical? Regions have to compete to do the best job for the people, and this would result in benefits such as high quality housing as a fringe benefit of living in a region.

Many science fiction books and movies portray a future where people live on spaceships, and housing is provided free for everybody on the spaceship. Why not create such a system on earth, right now?

Right now, roads are provided for everybody, and with the exception of a few toll roads, are free for everyone to use. Basic education is usually free for all. At least one country already has free healthcare for all, funded through taxes. Some regions will likely provide all the basics of life, food and housing, free for all, as a benefit of selecting that region to live in.

But this is not a requirement. There will be a lot of different regions and buildings, and some will certainly charge a lot of money to stay there, so everybody can have whatever they want.

A new economic system

Some new regions, built on undeveloped land, will experiment with different economic systems in order to find one that works better.

One of them will work better than the rest, and will likely get copied by most or all other regions.

This new economic system will be the system of the future, where nobody is left out, where everybody has a much higher quality of life than any other system could provide.

This is one of the benefits of regional competition. You would never see anything like this with the current system.

Limits

Ideally any group of people can form and run their own region. This is needed for a variety of reasons, especially so the regions have the consent of the governed.

However some people may not be responsible enough, and also we want to ensure a better future for humanity so we may wish to limit formation of a region to those who will do so with regards to a better future for humanity.

There may be some restrictions on who can start a region. For example, if three people get together and want to start a region, that is impractical.

A region is more like a city, or province, not a household.

Regions ideally should have a hospital, schools, a management building, and similar facilities.

There may be other restrictions on who can start a region, so we can be proactive in avoiding problems, as long as the restrictions are not excessive.

In particular, all children deserve a safe and good upbringing, so any prospective region with children may be required to show a plan to protect them.

If the region has only adults in it, that's different, but there probably won't be very many regions like that.

Anybody who is familiar with the Stanford prison experiment, knows there are aspects to basic human nature that need to be accounted for, when putting a group of people together.

It is important to be proactive when deciding if a group is qualified to run a region.

This will be one of the most controversial aspects of this project. To resolve it, we should hire people who have a high degree of intelligence and empathy, and have them research it.

Nature reserves

Some regions of land can be left to nature, nobody living there.
It might be a good idea to manage the land, maybe putting in firebreaks or doing other things that would help.

Other regions can be left to the indigenous people living there.

Extradition

Extradition is often abused. Regions must have the right to offer their residents protection from being extradited, especially if they have never even been to the region that wants to extradite them.

Research this subject on your own to see the abuses that are currently taking place, and you will see why we need to reform the international system.

Your ideas

Do you have any ideas of how to make a great region? Why not type up a description of your proposed region and promote it to see how much support it gets?

Have you ever wanted to run your own region? This is your chance.

This could help the project get started because it will get people interested in everything.

Remember to use a lot of enthusiasm when talking about your new region, because if you talk about it in a more boring or plain way then they will likely get bored with it and not support it very much. People really do respond with the same level of excitement as they are hearing, so it is a very good effective communication skill.

Another tip would be to point out how the region will benefit them or something they already care about. This will make a huge difference because most people have some things they already care about, and they are unlikely to take on something new.

It will be necessary to reference this book because the only realistic way we can get started is if we have enough people supporting it, and that means the alliance. The only way your region can get started is with the support of the alliance of all regions. A quick link saying your prospective region supports the proposal at www.endworldsuffering.org would be enough to get started. Disclaimer: no guarantee the alliance will support your proposed region, they may have some requirements as mentioned throughout this book, also there is no guarantee how long it will take before the alliance can be officially formed.

It could be really fun and satisfying to design your own region, especially if it gets enough support to become a reality!

How would you feel if you did form and run your own region?

Chapter 8:
Corporate regions

This could be the most objectionable part of this project, but there are some compelling reasons that we should consider this.

In the end, it is up to you to decide.

The question is do we let companies run some of the regions or not?

Advantages include the large amount of money they would invest into these regions, knowing they would get a return on their investment, which provides the investment we need to get started.

Companies know how to compete and improve themselves and offer you better service. That's why we use them today instead of having the government run everything.

If somebody doesn't want to live in a corporate region then they don't have to. There will be a thousand regions, some run by nonprofit organizations, some run by governments.

Phase out period

Money is the most powerful tool ever invented. We need to use this tool to get started.

Letting corporations run some regions might be a good idea. By letting them profit from regions, it encourages them to invest in them and get them started.

If we don't do this, then we run the risk of this project becoming another one of those great ideas that never went anywhere, only to be forgotten about as years turn into centuries.

Maybe we could have a phase out period, where they profit from it for 99 years, or whatever, then it turns into nonprofit. This way we get started quickly, and end up with a more equitable society in the end.

In the future, machines will be making all the products in unlimited quantities anyway, so money is likely to be obsolete. Everybody will have a very high quality of life in the future, if we do it right. Else everyone will be unemployed. That is also up to you to decide.

Things change a lot over time. A couple hundred years ago, we didn't even have electricity, phones, television, airplanes, antibiotics, and many other things.

Who knows what it will be like after a couple hundred more years of innovations.

Voting

Most people already work for a corporation and they don't get to vote on company policy.

With this system of regions, you now have the ability to vote with your feet and move to a region that treats you far better than you are getting treated now.

Remember, nobody gets left out with this system, land is proportional for each regions population, and everybody gets to pick a region to live in.

Regions will make everything better for you and people you care about.

Most people will never have to move because everything will get better everywhere, that's how competition works.

You will get huge benefits and not even have to do anything.

Corporate regions might be the best places to live though, because they are run by more educated, informed and intelligent people who make the right decisions, causing the region to be a very good place to live. That and competition which rids the marketplace of anyplace that can't keep up.

The old style of voting, which everybody is familiar with, means choosing a leader who then often sells out to lobbyists or anybody with a lot of money, and the people end up suffering for it.
The new style of voting, which this book advocates, is

voting with your feet to select the best region to live in.

Old style voting gets you campaign promises which are often abandoned after the election, then promised again at the next election.

The new style voting results in regions having to stay good all the time, else people could move out causing the region to go out of business. It's like every day is election day. You could move anytime you want.

Other competing regions would likely offer to pay moving expenses to get people to move there, they will make it easy to move, knowing it helps keep them competitive.

The new style is much better for you and people you care about, and will give everybody a much higher standard of living.

A corporate region should not be obligated to let its residents vote for leaders or policies because many voters are not informed and will screw things up.

If somebody doesn't like this then they don't move to a corporate region. There will be plenty of government run regions they can choose.

And everybody in those regions can act surprised if the corporate regions turn out to be better places to live.

A nonprofit region that disallows the old style of voting could end up being even better than a corporate region, since the money stays with the people instead of going to the corporate shareholders.

The problem with the nonprofit regions is they might lack the funding necessary to get started.

Corporate regions cannot promise one thing to get people to move there, then do something else. The alliance acts as a consumer protection agency to ensure all regions keep their promises to people.

We will need to make sure that conditions are spelled out in plain language so everybody knows what they are getting when they select a corporate region. We cannot tolerate any problems, this is too important.

We also need to make sure that people do not have to select a corporate region out of necessity instead of by choice.

It is vitally important that we build enough variety of regions so everybody can select one that is perfect for them.

A survey should be taken to determine what type of regions people want, then those regions need to be built first.

We must get off to a good start, not make people choose between the present system and one that isn't that much better.

Regions are for the people, and that is how it should start.

Corporations may have the money to get this started, but they need to use that money in a beneficial way.

Ideally groups of people who want to form regions should be able to get government loans to form a nonprofit to start and run the regions of their choice. But if that doesn't happen, we need alternatives.

Remember, you still get to vote in corporate regions, you just vote with your feet.

Corporate region advantages

One of the advantages of corporate regions is that once we find a system that works well, we can stay with it, not keep changing it all the time.

One thing that is wrong with our present society is that its too easy to make new laws. Every year, more and more new laws are passed. Over time, everything becomes illegal, freedom is gone.

A good corporate region is like a picture, frozen in time, with no new laws every year. It starts good, and stays good, with freedom for all residents.

If somebody doesn't like freedom, they still have the right to vote. Vote with their feet, that is.

They can vote with their feet and move to someplace that doesn't have freedom, and they only hurt themselves by doing that. The rest of us can enjoy our freedom, not being burdened by those who don't care.

More corporate advantages

Stores treat customers better, because they don't want to go out of business.

A corporation running a store is the same as a corporation running a region. They both treat people better so they can stay in business.

Compare this with how you are being treated today.

Choices

Regions are all about giving everybody more choices. How many choices does the average person have today?

Why this is workable

A lot of organizations have tried to save the world in the past, but they were too small or the world is too big.

But if we let companies run some regions, the companies will promote this plan so they can get their region started and profit from it.

This way we don't have to do everything ourselves. It's decentralized, and it's like having a thousand companies helping us. That makes this plan much more realistic than other ideas.

Imagine having a thousand companies promoting a thousand regions, advertising, investing huge amounts of money. This project would be certain to succeed if it had corporate support. Then we all win. Assuming it is managed properly, for the benefit of the people.

And other groups that want to save the world are invited to join us, so we can be a large team. Charities and others are all invited to join the team. If we get huge numbers of people to support this project, then we all win.

There are a lot of reasons this can succeed, but not all of them are printed in this book, which is just a getting started guide.

Evil

Corporations did not start out for the purpose of being evil. They have to put profits first because if they don't then the competition will run them out of business.

Then the only companies we have remaining are the ones that are the most profitable. And the people suffer for it.

It is like an unintended side effect of the system.

How can we fix this?

If we let everybody choose a region to live in, and the best regions get the most land, now their priorities have shifted to doing the best job for all of us, because they are competing to manage more land too.

If a region tried to put profits first, then it would be a bad place to live, nobody would choose it, and it would go out of business.

So all regions will start doing the best for the people, and everything will get better everywhere!

Since this new system is better for people, giving people a better economy and more money, everyone will buy more things which means more profits for the companies. So we both win, people get more money, and companies get more profits too.

But this is not going to happen by itself. It will only happen if enough people want it to happen, and support this plan.

It will likely only happen in a few areas where people get together and help it to get enough publicity to get started. Then hopefully the news will spread and the project will expand.

It might take a long time before the whole world gets its act together. But everyone who wants this should have the option of moving to a region sooner, to get the benefits without waiting.

It will be like the exclusive clubs that already exist, the only difference is that you are invited to this one.

Today

Corporations already run much of the world today. They have so much money and power and influence that the average person hardly has any ability to influence things, at least on a major level.

The problem with this today, is that they put profits first, and people suffer because of it.

Would you like to change this?

If so, please consider the plans in this book, either with or without corporate regions. We could do this without corporate regions if you and enough other people support it.

It really is up to you to decide. If you would like to do this without corporate regions, you can, but we will need to get a lot of public support for it. We will have to work hard to get this support.

Curiosity

I would like to think that enough people would like the goal of saving the world, and they would work to get this plan implemented.

But realistically, many people have work and family obligations, or other considerations, so they don't have the time or money to do this.

The good news is that if they at least support the corporate regions, then the corporations can make it work. Companies have the money to get this started, but they won't unless the public supports the plan.

So I would suggest that we first try to get government support for the project, to do this without corporate regions. If enough people want this then we could make it work.

If that doesn't happen, then we should consider the corporate regions. We could reward companies that support the plan by buying stuff from them, and boycott companies that don't support the plan.

Chapter 9:
Exclusive regions

Your existing society already has rich exclusive neighborhoods that exclude most people.

Regions give you the opportunity to live in an exclusive region, because any group of people can form a region and live there. You could join an exclusive region.

Exclusive regions are safer for your family because they allow you to exclude troublemakers and criminals.

One persons rights end where another persons rights begin.

People should have the right to live in a safe region with no criminals and troublemakers in it.

If a troublemaker doesn't like exclusive regions, then he can form his own region, and live with the other troublemakers where they can rob and victimize each other.

There will also be plenty of public regions that let anybody in.

The people will decide how many exclusive regions there are. If half the population wants exclusive regions, then half the regions are exclusive. Everybody gets exactly what they want.

Ideally every region will have an amount of land proportional to how many people choose to live there, so nobody is getting an unfair advantage.

Exclusive regions have the right to restrict immigration, or even to deport anyone who is causing problems.

Chapter 10:
Alliance details

There have been countless previous attempts to save the world, yet problems remain, and some are getting worse. Part of the reason that previous attempts didn't work is because they didn't have enough people, enough support.

To avoid that problem, and to make sure that this book succeeds, we need to form a global alliance of enough good groups. Such an alliance would be too large to fail.

Yes it can be difficult to get people to team up, but there are ways to fix that problem. There are plenty of examples, past and present, showing how this is possible. Nations and unions are only a couple examples.

Leaders

Current leaders can join the alliance, and still remain leaders, so we still have experienced people running everything.

Any changes will be implemented slowly and gradually, so there is no disruption to the existing system.

Oversight

We need a central organization to oversee the regions to help them get started, and to settle any problems in an intelligent manner. The alliance is this organization.

Wars

The alliance peacefully settles disputes between regions, so wars are never allowed.

Regions have to agree to this, in order to become a region.

After the whole world is converted into regions, wars will be a thing of the past.

This would save enough money to solve most of the worlds problems by itself.

Every region should contribute a small number of people to the alliance, to make a united team that enforces the peace. This is a lot better than the present system.

You can see examples today of people working together as a team for their common benefit, so all this is not unprecedented.

The team

One of the reasons these plans are practical enough to work is the large global team that will be the alliance. The alliance will not only consist of regions, it is any number of other groups that want to help save the world.

The alliance consists of regions, and groups like charities, and other groups.

It is well known that a larger team has more influence than smaller groups. Therefore we need to put together a global team of all good groups.

This team could become larger than any other team in history, which would give it enough influence to really get good things started.

All charities are encouraged to become members of the alliance for the purpose of helping it to get started.

Any good group should be invited to be part of the alliance, as long as it agrees with the goals of this book.

We must not allow groups to join the alliance for the purpose of trying to change it such that it puts profits first, over people.

Consumer protection

The alliance is like a consumer protection agency, it is responsible for making sure regions don't use misleading ads to trick anybody into moving to the region.

This way everybody still has the freedom to choose whatever region they want, but it is an informed decision that helps everybody choose a good region and have an excellent life.

Regions will also advertise themselves, and the news, internet, and word of mouth will serve as checks and balances.

Starvation

The alliance makes sure nobody starves, anywhere on earth.

While each region generally should grow enough food to feed everybody in their own region, some regions may be in climates that make that difficult. Droughts can happen anywhere periodically.

Also there are trace minerals needed in your diet, that may not be available everywhere, which necessitates having some variety of food from outside your area.

Normally regions trade with each other to get what they need.

But if some problem happens, then the alliance steps in to

make sure nobody starves. Every region should try to grow extra food, which is preserved, and made available to the alliance which distributes it to the region that is having the shortage.

If it is just a temporary problem like a drought, then the region can pay for the food, possibly over time.

If the problem is longer term, such as incompetence of the leaders of the region, then the alliance must step in and fix the problem.

It is in this way that no child will ever starve again, anyplace on earth. This is one of the many benefits of the alliance.

Animals

Animals should not have to suffer. They can probably feel pain just as humans can.

The alliance should require regions to ensure that no animals suffer within the region. Regions have to agree to this in order to become a region.

Once the alliance and regions are implemented worldwide, no animals will suffer ever again.

Do you see any other way that we could end the suffering and keep everything good forever?

Concerns

Some people may have concerns about the alliance starting out good, then getting worse in the distant future. These concerns may be justified, especially considering the type of world we live in today.

However we must consider the alternatives.

Look at the trend that is happening already.

Throughout history, people have formed larger and larger groups.

People formed villages.
Villages joined into countries.

Countries formed unions like the European Union, the African Union, ASEAN, and others.

In time, Mexico, America, and Canada will likely form a North American Union.

The next step, if this trend is allowed to continue, will be all the unions joining together into a one world government.

This bureaucratic mess will then make global laws, with nowhere to go to get away from it.

All the countries already make laws that apply everywhere in the country.

The unions are making laws that apply in every country

in the union.

The global government will of course make laws that apply everywhere on earth. Every year, more and more unjust laws will be passed, until there is no freedom left anywhere.

Do you really want an encyclopedia set of bureaucratic laws against everything you wanted to do, that applies over all of earth?

Such a system will then collapse, due to the corruption and bureaucracy, resulting in a global economic depression such that the world has never seen.

If there is even a small chance this will happen, then we must take it seriously. To do otherwise would be grossly irresponsible.

The only way to avoid this global bureaucracy is to form the alliance discussed in this book, which has regions of land that have their own laws.

The alliance only prevents wars between regions, and guarantees basic human rights like the right to move out of a region if you want to. It doesn't have the ability to make laws that take away freedom.

Regions are independent, so if one has a problem then it is confined to that one region. Decentralization works.

This is a far superior system, and is our only chance for global freedom and a good life.

The only laws against anything are in regions, and you can always move to a better region if you want.

Regions have to compete with each other for people to live there, else the region will go out of business, so you will not see excessive laws within any region.

The main point here is that we must write into every document regarding the alliance, that it must never be allowed to make global laws that take away any freedom. This must never change.

If anybody contradicts this, then they are not speaking on behalf of the alliance, and they should be ignored, even shunned.

This project to end world suffering is too important to be compromised by such people.

Majority rule

The majority make too many mistakes.

Majorities have voted into power such things as the prohibition of alcohol, and the loss of many other freedoms some of which persist to this day.

The majority has also supported slavery and all the problems resulting from that.

There have been a lot of other examples.

Majority rule may be better than some dictators, but it is still terrible for minority rights. Every time 51% wants to do something, the other 49%, the minority, loses yet another freedom. These mistakes are unacceptable.

Those mistakes will not be repeated with this alliance.

The alliance will never be allowed to make global laws that take away any freedom from all regions, even if the majority wish it (this refers to individual rights, not wars or anything like that which are a different story).

The alliance can and will prevent wars, because that protects peoples human rights.

The basic concept is that the alliance will never be allowed to take away individual rights within regions. The alliance is not, and will never become, a global government.

Everybody rules

The way we can fix the problems resulting from majority rule, is to let everybody rule, in the form of regions. This allows everybody to select a region that suits them, or to work with other people who feel the same way to make their own region. This way the majority can never again deprive individuals of their rights, which is something that happens a lot with majority rule.

The alliance exists to give people freedom and choices, not to take freedom away from people.

If a law is necessary then a region can implement it on its own.

Then there are other regions which lack the law, therefore freedom now exists for all people on earth.

The alliance must never devolve into a majority rule system that makes laws against individual rights. Regions are a different story. Regions can be run by majority rule if the people of the region want.

With this system, its *everybody rules* since everybody can select whatever region they want. Everybody rules is much better than majority rules.

With everybody rules, everybody wins.

Positive vs. negative

The alliance can't ban something worldwide, like the prohibition of alcohol, because that takes away the freedom to do something.

People do have the right to leave any region if they want. That is offering a freedom.

The alliance is only allowed to offer rights to people who want them.

The alliance is never allowed to make laws against anything that an individual wants to do.

The alliance does have the ability to enforce human rights

on a global basis.

The alliance will guarantee basic human rights to everybody on earth. This does not take any freedom away from anybody.

An example of a basic human right is the right to move out of a region.

Regions can jail people for crimes, but cannot jail somebody for wanting to leave the region, nor jail a large percentage of the people to prevent them from leaving.

The alliance should set a reasonable limit on the percentage of people that can be jailed, to prevent regions from jailing everybody to keep them from leaving. If the region wants to jail more people than the reasonable limit, then it has to allow the extras to move out of the region if they wish.

Regions cannot force surgery on anybody against their will, nor mutilate anybody. A person has the right to leave the region. It is a basic human right to be able to refuse surgery. If a person refuses to leave the region then that is a different case. In other words, a person owns their body. Regions may have local control, but basic human rights come first. This is extremely important.

Basically the alliance guarantees everyone the right to select a region where they will be happy, the right to avoid anything permanent like mutilation, and to be educated so they know their rights. The alliance handles these basics, and the regions offer more detailed rights.

This avoids any disagreements over the detailed rights, because there can be slight variations depending on the region. This way everyone can get the detailed rights they want, without having to impose it on anyone else against their will.

One of the biggest problems with the world today is too many things banned. This takes away peoples rights, and is completely unacceptable.

One of the objections to a world government is that it would make laws against something you want, that applies all over earth, nowhere to go to get away from it.

The alliance is not like a dystopian world government because it will never have the ability to do those negative things.

The alliance gives you the right to have a region where you can live with freedom, away from any unjust global laws.

Wouldn't it be great if you had more rights?

There will be a variety of regions, and some regions can be highly regulated for everybody who prefers such a system. So everybody gets what they want, this is called freedom, and it's good.

Future of the alliance

We must take steps to ensure that the alliance is never changed to have the ability to make global laws against anything that people may want to do. If we don't, then it will be no better than the system we have today.

The alliance can stop regions from having wars with each other. But it can't ever deprive individuals of freedom to do things that they want to do. If there is a conflict, such as something that risks injury to a child, this must be addressed, but the proper place for that is the meetings prior to forming the alliance, because there is insufficient space in this book for all of that.

The alliance must never be allowed to take freedom away from people, even if the majority wish it, because it is not majority rule, and this must never be allowed to change.

This is of vital importance.

An entire section of the alliance should be devoted to this guarantee, and every educational system should educate the people of the future to know why this is so important. The tyranny of the majority is over. Freedom is the way of the future.

This is a complicated issue, and will only get more complicated as new technology increases the ability of people to act across borders.

However all regions are part of the same global team, so the world really will be united. This is the how we fix the problem. We encourage everybody on earth to think and act as one global team, one big family.

We have friendship type activities all over the world, where we all share our new found wealth that results from the new systems in this book. We have so much fun that we don't want to do anything negative any more.

It is of the utmost importance that we make sure that the only people managing the alliance are those people with intelligence and a lot of empathy. Otherwise we will have a world of problems, much like we have today.

Branches

The alliance will have different branches.

One branch we could call the approval branch, which must approve anything the alliance does. It serves as checks and balances.

One important note is that the approval branch must approve it in advance, before it goes into effect, not declare it unconstitutional after it has already been causing problems for people.

The approval branch must consist of highly qualified people. A person must pass a psychological test indicating that they have a lot of empathy, as well as a knowledge test, before they can be in this branch. Only people who have a high I.Q. and E.Q. as well as empathy and knowledge, can work in this branch. We must never allow regions to turn this into some typical election/popularity contest, resulting in unqualified people getting in there. Perhaps we could give the psychological tests to candidates, then anyone who passes the test can proceed to the elections, so the result is people who are both qualified and elected.

Another branch of the alliance is the representative branch, where each region sends a representative to speak for that region. Most regions will likely hold a typical election to select their representative for this branch. Even though this branch will have a few unqualified people, it still represents the will of the people, thus has the important job of preventing injustices against the people.

Rights

People should not have to waste a lot of time researching all the details of a region before selecting one.

Everybody should be able to rest assured that every region will be free of hidden problems.

Its the same concept as when you go to the store and buy something, there is a reasonable expectation that the product is safe.

We must make sure that all regions have basic human rights. This includes a prohibition on torture, no matter what crime somebody is accused of. This is necessary because no system is perfect, mistakes get made, and we must never torture some innocent person by mistake.

It is also vitally important that no mutilation ever takes place. A person owns his or her body unconditionally. If an exclusive region doesn't like it then they can deport the person to a public region, but may NEVER force a person to undergo any surgical procedure against their will. The only exception is male circumcision since that essentially eliminates cancer of the area, so ideally that would be done as soon as practical after birth. Of course if it was skipped when the person was an infant, then it may not be imposed on anybody who is informed of the benefits but refuses the procedure.

Aside from that one exception, regions must be prevented from forcing any kind of surgery against a persons will.

This does sound like a conflict, since all regions are supposed to have local control, but it isn't because people have the right to leave a region.

Forced surgery and similar things, are something that people would likely regret, so the consumer protection agency (alliance) has the responsibility of preventing it. The person must have the right to move out of the region to avoid it.

Individual rights are of the utmost importance.

If we didn't do it this way, then some regions would probably have some situations where they punish people harshly, and most people would be unaware of it until it's too late. The alliance needs to prevent this, partly by guaranteeing the right to move out of a region to avoid anything permanent.

The problem is that many people are unaware of everything, especially when they are young, so it is our obligation to guarantee their safety and help them have a better future. It is the morally correct thing to do.

Some places seem eager to see somebody make a mistake, and then punish them harshly for it. That needs to be confined to the history books.

We need a more understanding future, a brighter future for humanity. A future system that puts more emphasis on educating people as to the mistakes they might make, so the mistakes can be prevented. Then everybody wins.

Language

Don't let anybody draw up documents pertaining to the alliance that are full of legal jargon, and loopholes.

Ensure it is in plain language so they won't be able to take advantage of people in the future.

Keep this book as the founding document.

Trade

The alliance cannot regulate trade between regions.

This can never be changed, else freedom would decline, and we would start to see incompetence happening.

We need to keep the world decentralized by using regions to run things.

To say again, the alliance can only offer rights to people, never take freedom away.

Idea

Here is an idea to make the alliance more effective.

Central planning usually doesn't work well, its too bureaucratic. To avoid this problem, the alliance will operate more like private companies, in a decentralized way.

For example, say a number of groups that have the same basic goal, join the alliance. Any of those groups can join together to form a team effort, which will of course be much more successful than a bunch of small groups that don't work as a team.

But this is not a centrally planned official branch of the alliance, with rigid bureaucratic rules that impede success.

The team is more like a private company, with its own self selected team members. It makes its own decisions on how to proceed.

The alliance may finance it, or offer other assistance, but the team has their freedom to operate much like a private company.

It is in this decentralized way that we can expect much better success.

Obviously those teams may not use the name of the alliance without permission, while promoting their goal. If the alliance feels the goal is good, and the team is not causing any negative publicity, then it may choose to declare it an official effort of the alliance, so the team can advertise with the name of the alliance.

The concept here is that we can avoid bureaucracy by allowing groups to team up to accomplish a goal, on their own. This is better than the alliance allowing only one project, and micromanaging it, resulting in failure.

The team will usually get support from the alliance, which is basically the same concept as the alliance subcontracting something.

Now we do need to have one large global team, that is the only realistic chance of success. Look at all those thousands of smaller groups that have come and gone over the years, failed because they didn't work as a team. But we can't swing too far the other way, and end up with a centralized bureaucratic mess either.

The main point here is that the alliance is not a rigid bureaucracy with one way of doing things.

It is more like a team that uses competition and freedom to achieve success. It pools resources where that is helpful, but it operates on a voluntarily basis wherever possible.

It is flexible and highly intelligent.

Division

Some people may question why we should divide the world into regions, saying it would be better to unite the world.

Yet we are uniting the world, with the alliance. All regions are part of one team, the alliance, so the world really is getting united with this plan.

Countries are already divided into states/provinces/cities and other jurisdictions, yet they are united as a country too.

It's the same thing here, just on a global scale. We are uniting the world while preserving individual rights.

Everybody on earth is invited to be a member of the alliance, with all the rights and benefits thereof. One global team. United, for the good of humanity.

Getting started

The alliance needs to make sure regions don't cause problems such as growing too fast resulting in being unable to take care of their residents.

There is a lot more to discuss about getting regions off to a good start, and making sure they stay good. The alliance will handle this.

Future of humanity

One responsibility of the alliance is to ensure a brighter future for humanity. It should be a leader.

One thing it can do is to identify problems and find a way to fix them. For example if cars are unsafe and resulting in a lot of people, including children, being hurt, then it should find a way to design the cars to be safer.

Considering the large number of injuries and deaths resulting from car crashes in many parts of the world today, this should be a priority.

It might cost more to make a safer car, but it is worth it. With the improved economy that results from regional competition, everybody will be able to afford it. In the future money will likely be outdated and not used anyway.

This is not the only example. The alliance needs to take the initiative and be proactive, not reactive. A branch of the alliance should have the task of seeing what problems might happen in the future, and prevent them.

Do you think the existing system will do a good job of protecting us from problems in the future, problems like a major meteorite strike?

Or do you think the existing system will wait until it is too late, like they usually do?

Genetic engineering

This could be potentially good or bad, depending on how it proceeds.

Anybody who is opposed to this should realize that it will probably happen anyway.

Gene therapy is already being used to treat some conditions in existing people. This is not the same as designing a new person, but it is mentioned to support the fact that it is possible to alter genes.

There are so many benefits of genetic engineering that it should be encouraged.

One of the good things about designing people, is that they can be designed to be free of diseases and unhealthy conditions. Every new person should have the right to be free from horrible painful migraine headaches, or any other problem. That should be considered a basic human right.

However there are a lot of possible problems, so we need to prevent any problems.

Since genetically engineered babies concerns all of humanity, it should be the responsibility of the alliance to prevent any injustices.

We need to make sure that the genetically engineered people of the future are not designed to be hard workers at the expense of being able to have fun. Nor should it swing too far the other way, with people who can't fix the machines when some technological failure occurs.

There is no reason we can't design people to be highly intelligent, while retaining the ability to have the ultimate pleasure too. Empathy for others should also be included.

It is not difficult to imagine some people of the future, engineered to be great workers, but deprived of the ability to have fun, with the result that they suffer a boring horrible life. This is unacceptable, and deprives these individuals of the right to decide the details of their own life, since their DNA is determined for them.

Now everybody gets DNA and has no say in it, but common sense indicates a healthy balance would be good.

Those of us who have experienced great pleasure, realize the value of this, and see the need to ensure the people of the future get to experience it too.

If we do genetic engineering properly, we could experience a whole new level of awareness. Some of you might already know what I am talking about.

On a less positive note, we should keep several groups of legacy people for a long time or forever, in case of unanticipated problems with the engineered.

It would probably be a bad idea to make everybody too similar in the future. Variety is good, for a lot of reasons.

The goal of genetic engineering or gene therapy is to make a future world where everybody thoroughly enjoys every minute of life, not taking things for granted, and is healthy enough to do so. And has empathy for others of course, so we can finally have a good universe to live in.

Wouldn't it be better to have people who thoroughly enjoy every minute of their lives, instead of having people who are so bored or miserable that they do bad things to other people?

It's possible that some people already have perfect or nearly perfect DNA, and that is fine, they can keep their DNA around forever.

But there are a lot of other people who suffer from problems that could be repaired.

A lot of people are self destructive and are a danger to humanity. The human race could be in danger of extinction because of such people, especially as technology advances to a certain point.

Chapter 11:
Machine labor

This has some good things and some bad things we need to look at.

Some people are opposed to the concept of machine labor, but it is already happening, and is expanding as we speak.

There are a lot of benefits to the concept of machines doing all the boring jobs, which frees people to work on more challenging things, or to have more time to socialize or do other things.

A lot of people would love to quit their boring job and get a much better job. This can happen if the boring job is done by a machine.

Some people would love to quit their job, and have machines do all the work, so they could live an enlightened fun life of being on vacation all the time, and still having a lot of money. Technology is increasing so fast that this is becoming an option.

Other people would be bored without a job.

We need a system that gives everybody what they want.

The past

If anybody is opposed to this, then they have to realize that a lot of automation has already happened, and much much more is on the way.

Ignoring this book won't change that.

ATM machines have replaced many employees at the banks.

A lot of cars refuel at pumps where you can put the credit card in the pump to pay and pump fuel yourself, this has replaced more employees.

Everybody has called companies and heard press 1 for this, 2 for that. Those computerized phone systems have replaced a lot of receptionists.

A lot of companies are replacing huge numbers of manufacturing workers with robots; enormous numbers of robots are already used on assembly lines.

As if that isn't enough, huge numbers of people are ordering products online, with their computers, thus replacing the humans that previously sold the products. So robots make products on the assembly line, then the products are sold online without human intervention.

It gets even better. Some companies already use wheeled robots to automatically pick the products off the shelves in the warehouse and put them in the box for shipping, once the computer has taken the order online.

It is easy to see what the future holds. Factories will be completely automated, with robots repairing other robots automatically. More robots will box up and ship the products when people order them with their computers. Robots will probably deliver the products too, at some point in the near future.

There are a lot more examples of automation.

The future

Even your job will likely be replaced, given the remarkable advances they have been making with artificial intelligence software and robotics.

Normally people lose their income when this happens to their jobs. What if there was a way to keep the money or the job?

One of the innovations you will see from the competition of regions, is that some regions will automate as many jobs as possible.

The way it works is the automated factories make products which are sold, and the money from selling the stuff goes into a fund, then your part of the money is sent to you in the form of a check or direct deposit to your bank account.

Since machines don't mind working double shifts every day, they make twice as much stuff, so you could get twice as much money as you are getting now.

There is already a lot of technology available right now, and more can be easily developed. Most boring jobs could be automated, now or very soon.

A self driving car has already been driven on the road, under computer control.

The money

Already in Alaska, every full time resident gets a dividend from the Alaska permanent fund which comes from oil on state land.

So it is not unprecedented for a government to give money to its citizens. All I am proposing is to give a larger amount of money, and to fund it from automation instead of oil.

And if you like your job, you can still keep it (regions have to be good to you in order to stay in business).

Note: before you move to Alaska, it should be pointed out that it is a remote area where many things have to be imported from a great distance, which costs a lot of money. It is more expensive to live there than in some other locations, and the dividend is not enough to make up for the cost increases. So the dividend is a nice idea, but is probably not enough reason by itself to move there. Before moving anywhere on this planet, it might be a good idea to research the jobs, crime, and other statistics.

The results of machine labor is that you can have all the money you need, without ever going to work. It could be like being on vacation and having fun all the time.

Imagine that.

If you don't care about that, could you please help us do this for the benefit of the rest of us?

Housework

Regions could easily fund the development of housework robots to do all the laundry and other housework, and clean the toilet.

Ideally these would be provided free for all, as a fringe benefit of living in the region.

If we don't make regions, how long do you think it will take before these become available or affordable?

The real reasons

It's not only about vacation time. Machine labor will free up people to develop more technology, feed starving children, and do other good things for humanity.

You may have noticed that the countries that use a lot of technology are the ones that have the high standard of living.

The ones without technology have the problems.

Imagine life without tractors. Subsistence farming leaves

no time to find cures to diseases like cancer, and improve life. Or have fun.

We need as much technology as we can get so we can accomplish the goals of ending world suffering and having more fun.

Machine labor is essential to accomplishing our goals.

If you do nothing, your job will likely be replaced too. Believe it, technology is advancing rapidly, even if you haven't seen it yet.

If you do nothing, your job may be lost sooner than you think, and most people in the world will not get any dividend check or other money. Even those lucky people who do get some money, whether it is unemployment benefits or whatever, will be getting far less money than they would if we do the plan in this book.

The reason we need to do this books suggestions, is not to automate jobs, that is happening anyway.

The reason we need to do this is so that we can still get a lot of money.

How would you feel if you lost your job, and were not offered a better one or enough money?

Technology is not going to stop, nor should it.

We just need to start getting the benefits from it.

Lets get those machine labor dividend checks going.

Question

Whether we like it or not, we are moving into a future where a lot of work is automated.

The question is what do you feel we should do about it? Are you prepared to tell huge numbers of people that it doesn't matter what they want?

Or do you feel it would be better to let everybody have what they want, by letting some people keep their jobs if they want jobs, and by letting some people live in fully automated regions?

The way things are going now, a lot more people will be unemployed in the reasonably near future, a number of years from now. If we keep things the way they are, what do you feel we should do about the larger numbers of unemployed people?

Dependence

It would be a serious mistake to become too dependent upon technology, and have some technology failure that results in massive problems.

We are already becoming way too dependent on technology in many parts of the world. Technology is good but if we depend on it, without enough backups, and it fails, then we will have no way to meet our needs.

So we need technology, but we also need backups for all critical systems. If we don't start taking this seriously, then there will be **serious** problems in the future, that will affect all of us.

Movie

If you are talented at film-making, and want to help this movement, then you could make a movie that graphically portrays an ultra-modern city that uses automation and gives the proceeds to the residents of the city.

This could help make you popular, as well as helping this movement in its goal to end world suffering and give everybody more fun than they ever thought possible.

Such a movie will help people understand these concepts much better than the brief summary in this book.

If you have time, include other concepts from this book in your movie.

Be sure to credit this book, since the only realistic way we will ever accomplish anything is by a large global alliance. Anything smaller probably won't work, as we have seen many times in the past.

Chapter 12:
Example region

This is just one example out of a thousand regions, so it will not appeal to everybody, nor is it designed to appeal to everybody.

This region will be built on undeveloped land so it can be populated by volunteers who choose to live this way.

This region is owned by the members, much like a credit union. You may have noticed that a credit union pays its members a higher interest rate on savings, compared to traditional banks.

The credit union also has other advantages over a regular bank.

Just like a credit union, this region is designed to benefit those who live there.

It is basically owned by, and run for the benefit of, the people who choose to live there.

Exclusive

This region is exclusive, and no troublemakers are allowed. If a person is untrustworthy and likes to rob or victimize others, then they are not allowed in this region.

This region will be populated only by responsible people, so if somebody needs medical assistance, somebody else will help them.

There are parts of the world today where people will step over or around an injured person, and not help them.

This region takes all steps necessary to avoid those problems. It offers free first aid training to everyone, so a lot of people will know what to do.

This region also makes sure that people are not hassled in any way for trying to help others. Quite the opposite, people are rewarded profusely for doing the right thing. Anybody who doesn't like this is not allowed in this region.

This is a region for team players, for the best people.

In some parts of the world today, there is a saying:
no good deed goes unpunished.

In this region, we have a saying:
no good deed goes unrewarded.

Applicants who want to live in this region have to pass a short psychological test indicating they are suitable for this region.

Anybody who is already in the region, but becomes unsuitable, is either deported, or possibly can remain in some sort of a supervised setting.

Medical

Residents of this region can go to any doctor they want, and the organization running the region pays the bill.

It's a fringe benefit of living in the region.

In some parts of the world they have private health insurance that is paid for by the employer. Those places usually have little or no delay when you need to see a doctor. The disadvantage is that not everybody has a good job, so many people get left out with those systems.

Other parts of the world give medical benefits to everyone, but a lot of such systems have lengthy delays to see a doctor.

This region combines the best of both systems. By giving the benefit to everyone in the region, nobody gets left out. Yet by letting everyone choose their own doctor, anytime, and ensuring there are enough doctors, we can avoid the delays. There are some details necessary to make this work, but regional competition will make sure that it works very well.

Basically this region is similar to the areas that have private health insurance, except that we give this insurance to everyone in the region. There are a couple other changes needed to make it work, such as a single payer system whereby the region pays instead of having a bunch of insurance companies.

In the future, there will be a lot of changes anyway.

There are already surgery robots, that are presently controlled by a human doctor, but in the near future the artificial intelligence software will automate the control.

The result will be a completely automated surgical procedure. Assuming we build enough of these computer controlled robots, there will be no wait time whatsoever for surgery.

And we will build plenty of them, considering they will be made in automated factories.

This region will likely be the place that the first such factories are situated.

Other tasks will be automated too, with the result that nobody has to wait for any medical procedure. And nobody gets left out.

We still have a lot of doctors for backup, in case there are problems with electricity or the machines. Or for those who prefer to avoid machines.

Presently, a lot of people are dissatisfied with the limited choices or the long wait time to see a doctor, so they become medical tourists. They go to another country to see a doctor of their choice and avoid the wait time. In this region that will not be necessary, we will have a lot of choices and a lot of doctors right here.

Economy

All the benefits of machine labor are in this region. We work to automate all boring jobs, for the purpose of having a higher standard of living.

This gives us more time for recreation or to move up to better jobs.

Since machines are doing most or all of the manufacturing, there are a lot of items available.

Some items are sold to people in the region, other items are sold to other regions.

Money from the sale of these items goes to a fund, which first pays for housing, and the extra is divided up and given to all residents of this region.

Because of this, housing is free for all residents. Nobody ever has to worry about making a mortgage payment or getting evicted or anything like that.

People in this region will never have to worry about the basics of life. Food, housing, and a few more things will be guaranteed just like basic human rights.

Manufacturing is not the only thing automated.

Small autonomous robots on wheels are used to deliver items like postal mail, and take the trash and recycling. They automatically drive down the corridors of the building at a slow speed, using sensors to stay out of the way of people.

This machine labor frees up time for people to work on other things so we can have the best life. This region will probably be the first to discover the cure to cancer.

This region will probably also discover the cure to the common cold, or flu, or other problems.

The organization running this region is dedicated to making sure every resident has the best life. It knows that it must do a good job else people will move to a different region and it will go out of business. It is run by residents who live in the region.

This region will have a very high standard of living. Once everything is implemented, including some things not mentioned in this brief introduction, people here will have a better life than they ever imagined.

This region will also have the highest life expectancy on the planet. People will live a long long time and love every minute of it!

Rights

This region offers every resident an impressive number of rights. Because every resident is responsible and trustworthy, we don't need to have a lot of restrictions.

Basically we can do anything we want as long as we are not hurting anyone else.

Safety

Most people will live in various high density buildings like the one described earlier in this book. They don't have too many rooms between the outer wall and the inner wall that defines the huge park in the center. Every residence can have windows overlooking the park, or the other side.

The building and the furnishings are fireproof.

The building is made of steel or some other alloy that is completely safe during earthquakes.

This region is a safe place to raise a family. Animals that may harm a child, are banned in this region, with no exceptions, regardless of whether it is some exotic animal like a lion, or any other animal that has ever killed or mauled any child.

Animals will not be needed for protection since we will have an excellent private security service situated in these high density residential buildings, as well as the fact that no criminals are allowed anywhere in the region.

If you have looked at crime and other statistics from around the world, you will notice that some areas are very safe to live, and others are not. This region will consistently have the best statistics on the planet.

It is not for everybody, but those of us who choose to live here should have the right to do so.

Every child should have the right to a safe upbringing, whether it is this region or not. The morally correct thing to do is to work for a future where this happens. The current conditions are appalling and need to be stopped. We can do better.

Some people may not wish to live in the high density buildings and naturally they have the freedom to live elsewhere. Every effort will be made to let people live as they see fit, as long as they aren't endangering anybody.

Food

One of the advantages of living in the high density building is the food. There will be several places to eat in these buildings.

This will be the best food in the world! Not only nutritious but also very tasty.

Right now, we have to waste a lot of time researching which food is healthy and good. It also takes a long time to prepare a great meal. The region will do that for us because they know they need to compete with other regions, so they will do the best job.

They will post the information for anybody to review and

verify, so anyone can see the details about the food.

This will be like eating at the very best restaurant in the world, every day!

If we cook and prepare food at home, this is rather inefficient. One person working for the region can cook a large batch in about the same amount of time, and feed a lot of people. Everyone can choose to eat in the galley, as they would call it on a spaceship, or perhaps the wheeled robots would deliver it to your door.

Of course everyone still has the option of home cooking.

But not everyone has the time to cook and prepare a meal that is both very nutritious and tastes great.

The galley here will make it very easy to get a great meal for every meal of the day! And it will probably be free of charge, for all residents of the region, just like some employers already give various free benefits to all employees.

Have you ever tasted the difference between fresh squeezed juice, and juice from a bottle? The fresh squeezed juice has a lot more flavor and nutrition. That's what the meals are like in this region.

Which one would you prefer?

It will be possible to give everybody great tasting food because we will use a lot of automation in the galley, which saves a lot of time for the people who work there.

Also most of the food is grown relatively near the building, then processed within the building. This is more efficient than trucking it long distances, as society does today. It also allows us to have food when it is fresh.

More food will likely be grown in greenhouses so we can have it even when it is off season.

All this food will be served without any potentially harmful chemicals like preservatives and pesticides.

Some of the food may be frozen but a lot of it will be harvested and served fresh.

There are a lot of other reasons why we can have the best and freshest food. One reason is the sharing of ideas and information so when a great technique is discovered, we can all use and benefit from it. It's another benefit of the teamwork of the alliance.

Another reason we can have great food is because the economy is better due to competition of regions. The improved economy means more money and more of everything including great food.

Dark chocolate is supposed to have some compounds that are very good for our health, although the usual processing methods destroy the nutritional value and reduce the flavor too. They also usually add too many calories to it, so we might be better off without it.

But I envision this region doing a better job, with less processing so there is so much flavor that they don't need to add calories.

The result would be a low calorie chocolate treat that we could enjoy every day, that is actually good for our health, and tastes better than any chocolate we have ever had!

Defense

In some parts of the world today, believe it or not, a victim is arrested if they try to defend themselves when attacked by some criminal.

This kind of learned helplessness will have no place in this region.

Even though there will be almost no crime in the region, no system is perfect therefore we can expect an occasional problem.

When a problem occurs in this region, a thorough investigation will take place and the victim will not be prosecuted for defending himself.

In some parts of the world today, criminals have more rights than everybody else. In this region, the reverse will be true.

Facial recognition

This is more of a problem in some parts of the world than others, yet it is spreading...

We have all heard news stories about people being in prison for decades before the person who actually did the crime confesses, and then they let the innocent person out of prison. Sorry about that.

Innocent people go to prison a lot more often than is commonly thought. Much of the time the mistake is never detected. This is unacceptable when considering there are better ways to handle this.

It is getting worse now that they are starting to use facial recognition software, which makes a lot of mistakes as it looks through all the drivers license and other photos to find a suspect. In my opinion, the improved versions of the software are still not reliable enough to justify ruining a lot of innocent peoples lives.

Eyewitness testimony is also deeply flawed. We have all heard news stories about mistaken identity and the like.

The fact is that a lot of people do look similar, therefore this region will not allow convictions based only upon appearance.

We can use more reliable methods to ensure that we prosecute the person who actually did the crime, which makes everything safer for everybody.

Remember, every time some innocent person takes the blame, that means the criminal is still out there victimizing people, and that is unacceptable.

How would you feel if you or somebody you care about was victimized by that criminal that was loose?

All because facial recognition put the wrong person in jail and allowed the criminal to remain out there?

The main point is that visual identification is deeply flawed, resulting in who knows how many thousands of lives ruined, and contributes to the high crime rate by allowing the criminals to remain free.

All this is unacceptable, and this region will be among the first to come up with a more intelligent way of handling it.

Static

We don't vote on changing things all the time. If somebody becomes unhappy here, they can move to a different region.

This is necessary to preserve this good lifestyle for future generations. There will be something written into the founding documents that it is not possible to replace these guidelines even if the majority wish it.

So it is not possible for people to vote to do away with the exclusive aspect of the region, resulting in allowing criminals to move in, for example.

This only refers to the guidelines regarding the type of region. We still have choices within the region.

For example each building may be run by its own organization so everybody has a choice without having to leave the region. This might be necessary at first while we work out the bugs. Once a great system is discovered and proven, then likely all buildings will be run the same way.

There are a lot of options and details. Please send the author an email at the address listed earlier in this book if you see anything you would like changed, or have any ideas to make things better. If something was not fully explained in this book, then that will have to wait until later, because this book is only a getting started guide.

Chapter 13:
Patents

The patent system is badly broken in many parts of the world today.

The alliance will never be allowed to implement a global patent system.

If some regions wish to use patents, that might be acceptable, but there should be some open source regions too.

This book was written by using open source software.

Open source often results in better quality, and lower cost. It has the potential to help everybody, thus it should be discussed in great detail. This also refers to open source hardware, and no patents on anything.

Reasons

Electric cars that don't pollute, would be more available and cost less, if not for patents that drive up the cost for electric cars today.

Imagine if you had an electric car that plugs in to recharge in 5 minutes. That would give it unlimited range, by stopping at fuel stations to plug in just as fast as refueling a standard car.

That is what everybody could have, if we use open source and cooperate over the internet to develop the technology, which everyone could use for free.

Maybe we could develop more efficient solar panels too, that don't use much energy to produce, so they could be manufactured in large quantities for a low price.

Regions that don't allow patents, that do allow free use of all technology, could have a far higher standard of living. If you research this issue on your own you can see many more examples and benefits.

Patents are outdated with todays technology and information sharing, where any idea can be worked on and spread worldwide over the internet.

Profits

If we decide to allow corporations to run regions, this might help everybody.

The old patent system allows corporations to profit on a product, but the new system of regions allows a corporation to profit on a whole region of land, which could greatly increase their profits, while improving the lives of everybody.

If corporations can profit from running the region, then they won't need patents any more. This can increase their profits because this system is more efficient. They might get less profit per sale, because the product isn't patented, but there will be so many more sales because the economy is so much better, that total profits for the year could increase. Also if a company is running the region then they can tax the sales or whatever, and get their money that way. There are a lot of options that are better for all of us.

Point this out to them and maybe corporations will help us all.

The first corporations to start regions will have their foot in the door, and can get a head start over the competition.

Standards

It is good to have standards.
Standardization keeps prices down because of mass production.

The alliance should set voluntary standards. Companies are not required to use them, but it could be to their huge advantage if they do. This will benefit everybody on earth.

It is acceptable to have regions respect brand names and trademarks with each other, especially since there will be a lot of trade between regions.

Slow

These patent changes may be phased in slowly and gradually, before everything becomes open source.

Regions and the alliance should pay programmers and engineers to work on open source software and hardware,

117

which is better for everybody. We can have the technology available faster this way, plus it is right to compensate everybody for working on it.

Chapter 14:
Conclusion

Do we the people have the right to self determination or not? If we do, then we should have the option to move to a region of our choice, and have a system that puts us first, so we can have a better life.

No more sweatshops anywhere in the world.

No more profits first, over people.

A lot of people on this planet are currently suffering under the tyranny of the majority, in a one size fits none. They have no choice, the economy is bad there and they cannot afford to move.

It is morally wrong to take the right to self determination away from people. Let everybody have the freedom to live as they see fit, in a region of their choice.

Freedom is the most important reason to implement the ideas of this book. The only way we can regain our lost freedoms is with the ideas in this book. This refers to economic freedom too, the ability to have more money and a higher standard of living.

Without regional competition, things will never get better.

Competition has been well documented to make improvements. We must start using it, in the form of regions that compete such that the better ones get more land, while the bad ones go out of business.

This will rid the world of problems that people suffer with today in many parts of the world.

Private charities are good, but it is a big world with a lot of problems, and it needs more than that to fix everything.

We need an alliance to oversee the regions to prevent them from having wars with each other, and to act as a consumer protection agency so no region tries to trap people there or violate any human rights.

The existing system has had its chance. Way too much time has passed, and world suffering continues. It seems obvious we need something new.

There are a lot of things in this book that should be clarified, and many more things that were left out, but we need to get started before too much more time has passed.

So let's start the alliance and get input from everyone who cares, to fix any problems, and work out all the details. Once we have a workable and detailed plan, then we can start to make real progress.

Cooperation

Since all regions are part of the same team, they will share information and ideas, which will help everybody.

We will see a lot of new open source projects which will benefit from the synergy. We will see hardware and other projects that result in free or affordable products and everything else.

The alliance should hire people to work on open source products, which will greatly help speed up progress. The sharing of information and ideas globally, helped and coordinated by the alliance for maximum effectiveness, will greatly benefit all of humanity.

One might think that regions would decline to share because they are competing against each other, yet sharing resembles a merger and has a lot of advantages.

Regions that share will enjoy the advantages, and attract more people, while reclusive regions may have problems and go out of business.

Companies will also share for the same reasons. Remember that companies can still profit from running the region, such as with taxes, so they won't need the old style of profits from patents and a monopoly and all that.

Goal

The goal of this book is to make a better future for humanity.

Competition and new systems will improve things a lot. Gene therapy and engineering will give us enough people who have the motivation and ability to have a good life, and they will improve things even more.

The world is what we make it.
Let's make it a good one!

We need a brighter future, and the ideas in this book are the only realistic way we can get it.

So if you like the idea of a better society, then let's get started! If not, then let's weep for the future.

www.ingramcontent.com/pod-product-compliance
Lightning Source LLC
Chambersburg PA
CBHW022010170526
45157CB00003B/1221